SOU FUJIMOTO

SERPENTINE GALLERY
PAVILION 2013

Sponsors' Forewords

HP is proud to be a partner of the Serpentine Gallery Pavilion 2013 and is honoured to be associated with the architectural visionary Sou Fujimoto. Fujimoto is widely acknowledged as one of the most important architects coming to prominence worldwide. He is the leading light of an exciting generation of artists who are reinventing our relationship with the built environment.

HP has a long and deep association with creative industries of many forms. Walt Disney was one of the company's first customers way back in 1938, using HP technology on Fantasia. More recently, we have seen the use of HP Workstations for enhanced editing at Abbey Road Studios, and celebrated the 20th anniversary of the HP DesignJet, a mainstay in creative offices across the world. We are very happy to be able to support the digital evolvement of the art industry and help drive the new ideas and approaches of tomorrow's industry pioneers.

Nick Wilson,
Vice President and Managing Director, HP UK&I

Hiscox is proud to be associated with the innovative and inspirational Sou Fujimoto, an icon in his field. We are also pleased to be able to support the Serpentine Gallery again; it remains a beacon of education and leading gallery for stimulating art. The Serpentine's annual Pavilion is one of my personal favourites and has truly earned its place as a highlight of the cultural calendar.

Robert Hiscox,
Honorary Chairman, Hiscox

Directors' Foreword

The thirteenth commission in the Serpentine Gallery's annual Pavilion series has been designed by Sou Fujimoto. Its translucent form, at once organic and geometric, presents a unique and sensitive response to the site and its surroundings. Fujimoto has completed a number of buildings in his native Japan, yet this is the first time he has built a structure in the UK. His built structures have focused on alternative ways of constructing both domestic and public spaces, blurring the boundaries between spaces, connecting spaces and forms in new and remarkable ways. Continuing these investigations, the design of the 2013 Pavilion was based on the concept that geometry and constructed forms could meld with the natural and the human.

The Serpentine Pavilion programme aims to offer audiences the opportunity to engage with the work of world renowned architects first-hand, in a uniquely intimate setting. Exploring the potentials for commissioning architecture, the Serpentine Gallery adopts an alternative approach, one that offers a very immediate process for the designers involved. Working in close collaboration with a team of specialists to realise the architect's vision for the project, the process of commissioning is only six months from invitation to completion. The series is unique worldwide and presents the work of an international architect or design team who has not completed a building in England at the time of the Gallery's invitation. The process of selecting the architects is guided by the core curatorial thinking of the Gallery, and in the case of this year's Pavilion was informed by Yuko Hasegawa, who first introduced us to Fujimoto in 2007.

The immediacy of the Serpentine Pavilion commission continues to provide an unparalleled site for architectural experimentation. Each Pavilion is sited on the Gallery's lawn for the summer months, operating as a public space and as a venue for the Serpentine's Park Nights programme of public talks, film screenings and performances running from June to October. We are delighted to present this catalogue to accompany the 2013 Pavilion and remain indebted to Sou Fujimoto and his team for working to create such an extraordinary and beautiful design for this annual Pavilion commission.

Julia Peyton-Jones
Director, Serpentine Gallery and Co-director,
Exhibitions and Programmes

Hans Ulrich Obrist
Co-director of Exhibitions and Programmes
& Director of International Projects

Contents

WITH PHOTOGRAPHS BY *Iwan Baan*

Kensington Gardens
Sou Fujimoto, 2012

This is the photograph I took last year during my visit to the Serpentine Gallery to begin this project. At that time I didn't know what I would make but this image clearly shows that I was unconsciously inspired by the site. With this Pavilion, I wanted to create something between nature and architecture.

Sou Fujimoto, London 2013

Sketchbook
Sou Fujimoto, 2012

For the 2013 Pavilion I have designed a translucent architecture, a terrain that encourages people to explore the site in new and diverse ways. Within these pastoral surroundings, the vivid greenery merges with the constructed geometry of the Pavilion. The inspiration for the design was the concept that geometry and constructed forms could meld with the natural and the human.

A simple cube, sized to the human body, is repeated to build a form that exists between the organic and the abstract, to create an ambiguous, soft-edged structure that blurs the boundaries between interior and exterior. Composed of fine steel bars, it forms a semi-transparent, irregular shape, simultaneously protecting visitors from the elements while allowing them to remain part of the landscape. The organic structure of the Pavilion overall is an adaptable terrain, encouraging visitors to create their own experience of the building.

From certain vantage points, the fragile cloud of the Pavilion appears to merge with the classical structure of the Serpentine Gallery, its visitors suspended in the space between the built and the natural.

Sou Fujimoto, London 2013

Various models for the Serpentine Pavilion 2013
Sou Fujimoto Architects

IN CONVERSATION
Sou Fujimoto with Julia Peyton-Jones
and Hans Ulrich Obrist

Julia Peyton-Jones: During the design process of this year's Pavilion we've gone from what we called, amongst ourselves, the 'Sugar Cube proposal', to where we are now, which is this very distinguished, very considered and very surprising design. What has this process felt like for you?

Sou Fujimoto: It has been a miracle! I got a lot of inspiration from all our conversations and discussions. Every little word and every little discussion made an impression. As you know, we started with the idea of the amphitheatre, then it kept changing and finally I met with you in my office in Tokyo. Through the discussions with you, I was gradually convinced of the direction it should go in. Of course, the requirements for the planning applications and the requirements from the Serpentine Gallery are very tight and this has been a good thing because you get feedback that has strengthened the ideas a lot.

Hans Ulrich Obrist: You told me in the *Now* interview[1] that the main point of your projects is never really the shape or the form of the architecture, but rather the various activities and behaviours within a space, as well as the relationship between its parts. And that's obviously very true of the Pavilion: it's a grid, it's a ring, it contains all these different relationships. Some architects just make a sketch – they have a form and it gets built. With you it's not that way. Can you tell us about your methodology?

SF: Of course, architecture is about making a space, an object, but the main point, the big interest of my architectural thinking, is to create a fundamental or new relationship between people in the space. For this Pavilion, the main programme is to make a space for people to behave in as they like. The amphitheatre was the clear starting point, but how to transform this rather formal structure into a more contemporary space, this was a nice challenge for me. The idea was to create a multi-directional amphitheatre – almost like an anti-amphitheatre. We started from a theatre-like space to create something …

JPJ: Like a bowl.

SF: Yes, like a bowl. At first it was a solid volume but then we thought it could be more like an anti-solid, like a ring but inside out, so that the solid wasn't solid any more. So it's not an amphitheatre any more; it's just a kind of field or a landscape, an extension of the beautiful lawn of the Serpentine Gallery, reaching to the trees. We tried to create something beyond the usual materials for walls and roofs, so these we transformed to more grid-like structures. The use of a grid is a classical method, but here the size of the grid changes so that it's not really a conventional grid, but more like elements to create a progression from outside to inside. Finally, we created steps – each step is 40 cm – which create small, transparent, cave-like areas or openings, a hole-like space. You can feel these structures as an extension of your behaviour. It's like a cloud. And there are different densities in the space: sometimes, if it's very dense, you can sit on it; it's hard like a body. But then when it's less dense, it vanishes into the air. People can reach their own understanding of the building through these differences in the distribution of density.

JPJ: The grid is a fundamental structure in your work; why did you choose the grid as the structure for this Pavilion?

SF: The first reason why we chose the grid was to escape from object-like things, so that there was a blurring of the line between the solid object and the space. I like the word you used in our previous conversations: you talked about 'meshing' different things with a grid, meshing nature and the Pavilion. 'Meshing' indicates different grids melding together, different geometries coming together, creating different things. At first, the grid was really rigid – a strict 40 cm grid – and I was a little bit worried about that because it was too regular. But then a nice thing happened, which came from the practical requirements of the structure. The construction team proposed an 80 cm grid instead of 40 cm and we made a model in my office with a combination of 40 cm and 80 cm grids that was much stronger because it created a more dynamic linking of these different densities. And then I understood that if we could combine these different grids, we could realise more closely my original intention to create different shapes, densities and spaces. It's more like the dynamism of living creatures, so it looks livelier than a strict grid. I like grids for this project because of their dryness, but at the same time they have this lively dynamism.

HUO: Why was the measurement of 40 cm important to you? Is that a golden measure?

SF: The main point is that people can sit on a 40 cm grid. It's more practical. Sometimes the choice of measurement can be really conceptual, but in this case it was mainly practical.

HUO: And the height of the Pavilion in relation to the Serpentine building, how did you judge that?

SF: That was quite difficult. I thought that the inner space should have a specific height, and gradually it grew and transformed in one desirable direction. It's like a bonsai tree: you cut the tree and then it grows in a certain way. In a sense, the design isn't determined by me; it's an interaction between the ideas and the model, the space and me and others, and then it grows and changes and finally becomes what it is. In that sense, I'm not a very conceptual guy; design decisions have more to do with a direct interaction with things.

HUO: The way you work with the grid made me think of the way Sol LeWitt deviates from the grid. There seems to be total reason in his work, but then there's also this irrational element; there's order but there's also disorder.

SF: The grid is a really strict order, but because of this strict order, we can mesh in nature and mesh in the behaviours of people. And because of the small size of the grids, the surroundings

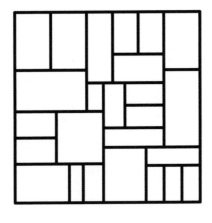

Sendai Hospital Annex, 1999

Children's Center for Psychiatric
Rehabilitation, 2006

come through, so it becomes softer, more interactive, and of course the shape itself follows that of the grids. It's really transparent, and because of this transparency, the blurring, the disappearance of the building into the surroundings is really strong.

JPJ: The thing about the Pavilion that I find fascinating is the degree to which you've used the grid to play with archetypal, particularly Japanese devices that frame the view. You frame the view in a very light way. Because the steel is only 20 mm wide – it's very small – there's a sense of drawing, as if you've drawn a number of lines around the view. And this goes back to how you use the grid in domestic architecture. A marvellous example is the Tokyo Apartment (2010). If you take the outline of that building and remove the content, what you've got is a plane cutting across a grid. Within these elements of lightness, there's a certain brutality, which is a word that's probably not very often associated with your work. Can you tell me more about this play between these light and brutal elements?

SF: In the case of the Tokyo Apartment, I played with the frame inside and the shape or the form outside. There's a nice ambiguity that creates the depth of the experience. With the Tokyo Apartment, I deliberately intended to create a strange encounter between two different orders, or order and disorder. With the Pavilion, although the whole shape is made from grids, it's ambiguous. It began more like a round shape and a smooth surface, but I tried to destroy that a little bit. There's no clear encounter of different orders and different worlds – it's more as if different things are melding together, and both the grid and the shapeless form remain quite pure, even though there's a co-existence.

HUO: Very often, a lot of the work of an artist or architect is already there in the first piece, and it's interesting if one looks at the first building that you designed: an annex for your father's psychiatric hospital. Here again, there was this play between order and disorder, and

Landscape in Hokkaido
Sou Fujimoto

Tokyo street
Sou Fujimoto

the idea of the ring is also already there. Could you talk about how these ideas had already manifested themselves in that very first building?

SF: Yes. It was almost twenty years ago and at that time I was interested in the theory of complexity and the theory of order and disorder, which I read about it in books by Ilya Prigogine. In my schooldays I was a big fan of Le Corbusier and his ideas on rationalism and precise order and the Unité d'Habitation in Marseille. Then after that I got into theories of complexity and I thought it was time to think about something beyond a Le Corbusier-like order – a mixture of order and disorder. Then I got a project from my father for a psychiatric hospital, and that's another one of those order/disorder things, because mental diseases are a kind of a disorder, while hospitals for mental disease are very ordered. My father wanted to get away from such a strange situation, and back to a more normal living situation. So I tried to find a really simple solution, but still with order, using a ring-like form. According to the logic of a hospital, every space should be exposed, so that from one point of view everybody can be seen; but with a ring, there's at least one point where patients can't be seen. My intention was to create a hidden point for people, a protected point. Order, disorder, simplicity and complexity: there's a nice co-existence of the different things that have been my themes ever since.

JPJ: It's interesting that this idea of the labyrinth has been running in tandem with the grid in your work, was a starting point in your first building and has been important to your thinking ever since. Perhaps it is partly because of the influence of Tokyo on your work – which on the one hand has this incredible discipline, with its grid of narrow and wide streets, and on the other hand as a counterpoint, these random, anarchic loops of telephone wires that link one place to another, which I find endlessly fascinating. The idea of the labyrinth even occurs within projects that are quite modest in size, like Final Wooden House (2008). You've managed to create this way of having a public space and also numerous private spaces.

SF: Maybe that comes from my experience of Tokyo city. I'm originally from Hokkaido and that area is countryside, so the house is your territory and if you go outside, it's just nature; it's not that it's your enemy, but it's something like that. But when I moved to Tokyo, there was more of a blurring between inside and outside. I found such a mixture of private and public areas the exciting thing about Tokyo's small spaces. As an architect, it's a good chance to challenge such a fundamental aspect of architecture, creating these spaces between public and private, rather than strictly dividing them. This is another really fundamental part of my architectural thinking. Even with a private house, I'm not just thinking about making a home, but about how to create an in-between space and how to produce this resistance point between private and public. Sometimes a small private house can have other meanings.

HUO: This could be a model for thinking about bigger things in terms of collective housing and social housing. There's a lot of discussion right now in Japan and elsewhere about this idea that given the economic situation and given the lack of resources in the world, there's more and more necessity for sustainability. The idea of having a bigger apartment

House NA, 2011

of your own becomes obsolete and the whole notion of shared spaces, collective housing and collective living becomes more relevant. How could these ideas that you've been talking about be applied on a bigger scale to collective apartments or social housing?

SF: I'd like to have the chance to apply it to bigger scales, but unfortunately I don't have such a project at the moment. But yes, in my early days I made a small plan for a new type of lifestyle in Tokyo. It's very common to have a small space with little rooms in the city of Tokyo, and then it was my idea that you could connect to the city by way of pathways. So your house is not only the one box, the one object, but is spread out across an area, a territory. Then different houses would overlap each other, so that you can meet certain people every morning, for example. In this case there's no form; it's the concept of a network to create experiences in life. I think we can push and update such an idea to create even more order and disorder, through Tokyo-like architecture and collective housing.

JPJ: So you'd have in one space, let's say, your living area and then in another place in the city you'd have your bedroom and then in another place in the city you'd have your kitchen? This is fantastic because then the looping of the electrical wires, these drawn lines around the city, could link in a metaphysical way, drawing a line between the spaces to make this kind of connection. It comes back to the idea of the labyrinth, and I would even say the promenade. How does this work within urban planning and control and maximisation of space?

SF: In Tokyo we have House NA (2011), with its many, many steps. That's a small house in Tokyo with a small site. So we talked with the client about dividing the small site into much smaller

Transparency study
Sou Fujimoto

pieces and extending each room over different levels. Then you can easily combine two different levels together to create the one space, or three or four different levels to work as a combined space. We have nice gradations within this private house, and richness is possible in such dense situations.

HUO: To return to the Serpentine project, I want to ask you about the influences behind your Pavilion. Who are your Japanese influences?

SF: I'm very lucky because I'm working in the context of such a continuous flow of architectural influences. Of course, these influences are sometimes too strong, so it's really hard to go beyond them. But Toyo Ito and Kazuyo Sejima are really supporting the younger generation. As you know, in Japan the traditional architecture or the traditional culture is ambiguous and complex, and in a mysterious way Fumihiko Maki's form is the clarification of such ambiguities. I myself am very interested in such Japanese traditions. At university, we studied architecture by Le Corbusier and Mies van der Rohe, not Japanese traditional architecture. It's strange, but as a result traditional Japanese architecture seemed very exciting to us because it had a distance from our architectural education. So I tried to understand and translate our traditional culture but in a way that's different from our contemporary culture. Then I read some books by the Japanese composer Toru Takemitsu, who combined Western classical music and traditional Japanese music. So my influences have not only come from the architectural field, but from music, culture in general. I read books by foreigners like Roland Barthes about Japan and then I tried to translate this back to my own culture. And through that process I became influenced by the work of Kenzo Tange and Fumihiko Maki because they did the same thing in a different way. And of course from SANAA I learnt a lot about how to re-translate Japanese traditional scenes. So we have the continuity of the Japanese culture, and we try to understand both Western architecture and our traditional cultures.

JPJ: Talking about Japanese tradition or Japanese culture brings us to the garden and to nature. The Serpentine is of course in a large garden, Kensington Gardens. You've described the garden as being the primordial form of architecture, so how does this context inform your Pavilion – if at all? It could be that the Englishness of this context is so foreign to the Japanese tradition that you can't necessarily relate to or engage with it.

SF: Yes, the Japanese garden is an inspiration, because it is of course nature, but it's also carefully designed – landscape design or architectural design or environmental design. For me personally, I like the contrast between the garden outside and architecture inside, while both have a similar role in our lives: influencing the behaviour of people. Considering how the covering of architecture is the strongest limitation in architectural thinking, I thought that if we removed the roof, a building could become a garden. I always try to make gardens a point of comparison to architecture – to show the differences or the similarities, the mutual influences that each has over the other. The landscape is quite important in my architectural thinking, and I'm very interested in and inspired by Japanese gardens, so I try to extend such landscape-like things into architectural forms. The Japanese garden is quite complex but allows for individual experiences and unexpected vistas. I like to take such complexity into architecture. With the Pavilion I was thinking in this way. To create sloping areas would be a too direct an interpretation of the landscape-like thing, but creating soft territories and soft articulations, gradually changing atmospheres and functions that emerge through experience or through the behaviours of individuals – such an understanding of the landscape influences this Pavilion a great deal.

1 Sou Fujimoto interviewed by Hans Ulrich Obrist, Venice Architecture Biennale, 2010.

House NA, 2011

ON SOU FUJIMOTO

Niklas Maak

An unusual house stands in a quiet side street in Tokyo. The first, shocking glance gives the impression of a house that has lost its clothes: wherever you look, there is not a wall in sight, nor does it seem to have any floors. There is hardly any furniture, and where such items do exist, they hang around like irritated tourists who have taken a wrong turn. The house stands in the street like an idea that is just in the process of taking shape – and in this process the customary notion of the home dissolves. House NA replaces the house with which we are familiar: a sequence of 2–4 metre high equally sized stacked boxes, connected by stairs or a lift. In their place is an ingenious, irregular suite of plateaus that ascend like so many stairs. Where once there were four storeys, now there are twenty levels, all complexly interlinked. The house resembles a climbing wall in which there are niches for children to play and adults to bask in the sun and drink tea. And where once there were walls, now there is glass; House NA consists only of window frames, with curtains providing privacy. At every turn there are hidden compartments and open levels on which you can sit, exposed as if on top of a cliff jutting out over the ocean.

Models for House NA, 2011

Many of the projects masterminded by Sou Fujimoto, who was born in 1971 in Hokkaido, Japan, seem so light, so clear, so refined, that you would be forgiven for thinking that gravity has ceased to exert its pull. Parts of his buildings float in space as if they were frozen moments of the slow-motion explosion at the end of Michelangelo Antonioni's *Zabriskie Point*. House NA's elegance stems from the fact that it seems impossible that it could exist: its load-bearing columns appear far too slender. Although constructed, it continues to resemble a computer drawing, a built optical illusion. The mass of concrete, stones and glass manage to retain the magic of the first design proposal (which with other designers always seems more elegant and lighter than the realisation), while sustaining a utopian balance between the intellectual construct and the actual building, projection and object.

House NA also answers the question of how, on the smallest of footprints, inhabitants can be offered something hitherto only to be found in far larger buildings. And this is an urgent issue. According to a Deutsche Bank study, in order to absorb the growing population in the world's conurbations, almost one billion new apartments need to be built by 2030. Even if this figure is an exaggeration, according to UN-Habitat, the UN initiative for human living, today 400 million city-dwellers live in homes that are critically overcrowded. It will simply not be possible, economically or ecologically, to fill housing needs with the usual arsenal of tools and forms preferred by architects and urban designers. So what will the houses and apartments of tomorrow look like? Who will populate them, and how? What will constitute a home, what will the notion of privacy mean?

The word 'house' invariably brings to mind walls, doors, furniture. If your brief is to design a three-storey house, you inevitably think of stacking three boxes, each with a ceiling height of about 2.70 metres. As House NA shows, Fujimoto takes a different tack. He deconstructs the notion of storey and floor, and is thus able to imagine what could happen within the total height of three 'floors'; how to stage the space, for example, on twenty different levels.

Ryue Nishizawa
Moriyama House, 2005

Instead of first working with shapes, Fujimoto starts with an inquiry into language. What can a 'storey' represent? What constitutes a 'public space' exactly? If architecture, as a rather conservative medium, endlessly repeats given spatial concepts, this lack of invention has a lot to do with linguistic issues. Fujimoto questions the categories usually taken not only to describe, but also to conceive architecture; the formal freedom of his architectural thought is rooted in this critical attitude towards the given. In his buildings, an aesthetic of porosity prevails, if we understand 'porosity' to mean ambivalence, permeability, changeability and the relaxation of strict spatial categories. Fujimoto liberates architecture from the iron cage of concepts that prevent its development and hinder its possible versatility and diversity, its reinvention.

Contemporary Japanese architecture offers countless examples of such formal thinking beyond traditional concepts of space. Other buildings worthy of mention are Ryue Nishizawa's Moriyama House (2005) in Tokyo or ON Design Partners' Yokohama Apartments (2009). Moriyama House resists both the notion of 'house' and that of the 'mini-city'. On behalf of a developer who only wanted to build two houses, one for himself and one to rent out, Nishizawa came up with ten freestanding hotel suites; the owner lives in three of them and rents out the others to tenants. The ensemble of ten white residential cubes succeeds on all the points where the flat-share communes of the 1970s failed. It offers a kernel of the private and the intimate, while inventing new types of shared areas: the roofs, communal patios and corridors morph into gardens, all in the middle of the city. Fujimoto takes this idea and gives it an

Model for House before House, 2009

Final Wooden House, 2008

even more radical twist; his House before House (2009) stacks residential cubes that are barely the size of rooms to create an artificial cliff. He then places trees between them and has the inhabitants climb up the structure as if moving between the branches of a tree. The house intensifies sensory perception by dragging nature into the city, truly creating a residential landscape.

Fujimoto's Final Wooden House, which was built in 2008 in the woods of Kumamoto, is likewise a *denkgebäude* – an edifice of thought. It is a cube with a footprint of only eight square metres, inside which ingeniously stacked 35-centimetre-thick beams create a spiral surrounded by protruding wooden elements. You can sit, sleep, watch TV, etc., on the various levels – in other words, do what is customarily termed 'living' – but there is no furniture, no walls, no doors. The protruding beams substitute for furniture and are completely versatile, possible uses range from a table, to a sofa when covered with cushions, to a bed when covered with mats. Here, the entire range of objects and concepts associated with a dwelling become superfluous. The house subverts the terms used to describe and construe architecture. Anyone planning a house automatically draws rooms, walls, doors, spaces for the furniture. Fujimoto shows that things can be done differently. Final Wooden House has nothing of these normal characteristics of a house, but it is inhabitable all the same.

The same is true of Fujimoto's House N (2008) in Oita, which resembles a Russian Matryoshka doll – the structure is composed of several fenestrated building skins, ingeniously

House N, 2008

superimposed one over the other, which are in part open and in part covered in glass. House N is not a hermetic object, but more like a stage. It is porous in many respects. It softens the harshness of the smooth wall by admitting exterior space, transforming the wall from a simple separating device into a three-dimensional spatial object. The boundary between inside and outside space consists not only of one wall, but of a series of walls and spaces. This transformation of the straightforward 'curtain' wall into a space-encompassing, sculptural entity questions any categorical distinction between 'space' and 'wall'.

Fujimoto's buildings incorporate classical elements of traditional Japanese architecture, such as the idea of the veranda-like *engawa*, or the classical Japanese room divider, the *shōji*, which enables houses to be adapted to various uses as required and which allows residents to repeatedly redefine the line dividing indoors from outdoors. In this sense, Fujimoto's designs are firmly in the lineage of architectural spatial inversions in which rooms fail as classic interiors but are transformed by a flexible turn of thought into successful outdoor spaces, while keeping a subliminal atmosphere of intimacy. One of the most famous examples is Piazza Jacopo della Quercia in Siena, Italy. After several failed attempts to build a roof over the aisle of the Siena Cathedral, whose walls were already standing, a decision was taken to redefine the three inside walls as outside walls and thus transform the inside of the

Piazza Jacopo della Quercia, 1339–48

transept into a plaza. In this way, the space now resembles an architectural reversible jacket; the interior becomes the exterior, the failed space, the basis for a possible new spatial experience.

A more recent example of flexible spatial inversions and the breaching of architectural categories is the chapel of Notre Dame du Haut in Ronchamp, France, completed by Le Corbusier in 1955. A close look at the east front reveals that both the inside and the outside are designed like an interior wall. Both have an altar, a pulpit and all the niches, platforms and fittings required by the liturgy. In this sense, there is no outside wall. Into this wall with two inside facades Le Corbusier installed a glass case containing the old statue of the Madonna on which the local cult of the Virgin centres. Visible from both sides, the figure is mounted on a rotatable pedestal fitted with a crank. When the Madonna gazes out into the landscape, the chapel's exterior is defined as an interior: the faithful gather outside the church, and the interior now consists of the hill and the rest of the world. This trick, easy to justify in liturgical terms, is but one example of Le Corbusier's method of abolishing spatial hierarchies, something with which he had already experimented in the late 1920s in his Villa Savoye. Floating in the landscape on top of *pilotis*, the house is entered from below, the visitor ascending into the living area, invalidating all notions of 'front' and 'back'. At Ronchamp, Le Corbusier took this erosion of customary distinctions one step further, to include a more open and interactive definition of inside and outside. Fujimoto's blurring of spatial categories might well be seen in this tradition.

Le Corbusier
Notre-Dame du Haut, 1950–5

In a theoretical treatise, Fujimoto has listed ten themes for a new art of the spatial, including the nest, the forest, the grotto, and the *guru-guru*, or spiral: a construction typology that seeks to present different spatial models taken from nature to create space. His built 'forests' resemble tree canopies, in which the inhabitants create their nests. In a presentation of the elementary gestures of building, four walls are erected around a tree, which then finds itself as captive of the space, creating a *hortus conclusus*, where nature becomes a garden and thus private. He designs houses that rise up from ever-denser thickets of wooden staves, houses that tower up from stacked wood (such as the Final Wooden House) and houses that arise by sinking a shaft into a block.

A line can be drawn from Fujimoto's interest in the motif of the spiral to Le Corbusier, who not only collected pristine shells as examples of nature's unsurpassable mathematical harmony, but also gathered hundreds of split and fragmented shells, cracked pieces of driftwood and abraded bricks. They were either distorted artefacts – such as bricks that, having been fired by human hand, fell into the sea and were transformed by the action of the water from a rectangular block into a smooth ovoid shape – or they were natural objects that somehow looked treated or constructed, like broken seashells whose helixes appear to have been turned inside out to reveal their structure. When such objects are split open, it is impossible to say exactly what is interior and what is exterior. Established ways of describing space dissolve. However, Fujimoto shares with Le Corbusier more than just a preference for spiral seashells and for smooth white surfaces: he also aims for spatial openness, a notion that ultimately results in a different concept of the architectural object.

Fujimoto takes the elements of architecture apart, as it were, and re-assembles them in a more leisurely, freer vein, as a landscape, a stage, and not as a hermetic sculpture. This is where his buildings differ fundamentally from traditional buildings and their logic of the 'spaceship', where it is a matter of life and death to know the inside from the outside: inside is where you find the air to breathe, outside is everything else. The logic of the spaceship defines the outside as an inimical zone. Perhaps the success of the spaceship buildings has something to do with a fundamental change in our relationship to public space, which has morphed from a promise into a problem, a space that is primarily shaped by rituals of control and enhancing efficiency. In the 1970s, the foreign, the stranger, the so-called 'other' was a screen for projections of the greatest flights of fancy, whereas today it is a domain associated more with violence or dangerous diseases. In an age when the relationship to public space is above all shaped by efforts to impose security from above, Fujimoto's architecture involves a different take on the outside world. His buildings are more open, more labyrinthine, more porous, more interwoven. He invents new spaces in order to change forms of social coexistence, for new rituals of being alone and being with others.

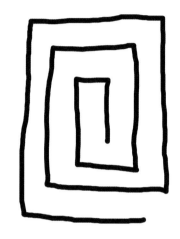

Drawing for Musashino Art University
Library, 2010

So what effect does this dissolution of the hierarchical categories used to separate the inside from the outside have on the question of the private sphere and identity? Put differently: what significance do Fujimoto's buildings have in an age in which the notion of the private sphere is radically changing, on the one hand owing to the virtualisation of the public and our embedding in social networks, and, on the other, due to the greater degree to which, through data evaluation, technical surveillance and monitoring equipment, our private lives can be spied upon? It is an age in which the concepts of private and public have perhaps lost much of their descriptive force as binomial opposites. What does private or public even mean today? When someone who has sat for seven hours in a private room sending emails and text messages, Skyping and making telephone calls, then goes out on the street without his smartphone, as he is stepping out of the private into the public or vice versa?

Model for Musashino Art University
Library, 2010

If differences between inside and outside, private and public are becoming eroded, what does this imply for the house, the plaza, the city?

When leafing through magazines devoted to home interiors, one can perceive a current trend toward immersive comfort in dwellings, the intention being to lock out or erase the chaotic world. In Fujimoto's oeuvre, private and public are structured differently. Here, the threshold between inside and outside essentially involves a deep spatial labyrinth, in which their relationship is playfully balanced. Fictitious space also plays a role here, as with the *trompe l'oeil* in House N. A borderline is more effective if the intruder loses his bearings. The many-layered filter, the labyrinth, functions better in this regard than does a wall, which once scaled allows the intruder to penetrate to the heart of the place. This elision of restrictive limits within the depths of space can provide far more effective protection for the inner life than thick walls and doors, as can be seen in traditional Arab architecture. In the age-old shops-cum-houses in the Maghreb, the first filter is formed by the wares placed in crates one next to the other, leaving only narrow aisles leading to the storeroom. The latter is itself a deep labyrinth that sometimes leads to a kitchen. There is not a single door between this private chamber and the street and yet the inside is much more effectively protected from the outside than by the average door, which could easily be broken down.

This doctrine is to be encountered in House N, where the spatial depth of the filter zone first creates a sense of non-claustrophobic homeliness. The relationship between public

Street in the souks of the Medina
Marrakesh, Morocco

House N, 2008

and private spheres is filtered here, and there is a room for every meteorological situation or emotional state: open, semi-open or completely closed. In traditional Japanese architecture, the *engawa* is such a space, a flexible interstice that can be changed, depending on how you open or close the sliding panels between street, garden and interior. This diversity of space is a key quality of most of Fujimoto's buildings.

In his theoretical writings, Fujimoto distinguishes between nest and cave as fundamental typologies for dwelling. The nest is not a pre-existing structure, but must be created in accordance with rational viewpoints as a response to a precise need for a home. By contrast, the cave pre-dates its inhabitants. Here, the inhabitant's achievement, his architectural act, is to discern that the existing cave is inhabitable and make his lodgings there. This act of *einrichtung*, of *sich-einlassen* is fundamentally different from the act of erecting a building. The inhabitants of Fujimoto's building are thus active, rather than passive, since Fujimoto (and here he is possibly a contemporary Mannerist) has a talent for building houses that have to be conquered every day anew, like a cave, like pre-given nature, and in a more playful and freer way than the act of dwelling usually entails.

Fujimoto's staircase of staggered seats designed for the Venice Biennale 2010, based on a model from 2001, is precisely such a form of architecture, as it is essentially an abstract landscape continually waiting new types of temporary settlements. It seems like an echo of the experimental residence devised by Claude Parent, the utopian French architect who, back in the 1960s, sought to find out with his own house in west Paris what happens if you

Model for Primitive Future House, 2001

take away from a house the very thing with which you always start when drawing: the straight floor, the level foundations. For this reason, the Parent family lived on ramps covered with dark carpets. To eat they lounged on recliners, setting their crockery down on triangular table-like objects. Parent hoped that social relationships, the dynamism between people, would change, become better, more exciting, less formal, if the even floor was pulled out from under their feet and rigid chairs whipped out from under their behinds. Both his and Fujimoto's living interiors are examples of a belief that architecture can influence social relationships, encourage or prevent certain forms of behaviour.

Fujimoto's Serpentine Pavilion should also be read in this context: as a social machine in a moment in which public space is more and more shaped by commercial interest and consumerist actions, the Pavilion offers a counter model for a contemporary public space, a stage, an open, inclusive framework for a new form of collectivity and urban experience. From afar, its shape reveals nothing about its scale. There are no windows or doors to show how large it is. It could even be a house-sized model of a futurist city in the clouds, such as those designed by Japanese Metabolists like Arata Isozaki in the 1960s – or one of Yona Friedman's utopian superimpositions.

Model for Ordos 100, 2009

This oscillation between model and house, pavilion and city, brings us to another interesting question: what would Fujimoto's light, open, labyrinthine yet inhabitable architectural landscapes that defy all categories of inhabitation be like if built, not on the scale of a house, but of a city? What would a neighbourhood look like that obeys the same formal laws as the residential cliff, the caves and the nests that his houses offer us? What happens if the categories used to describe and construe public spaces and cities are taken apart in a manner similar to what Fujimoto does to the notion of domestic architecture? This question serves to expand the field of architecture and dwelling into the sphere of the *res publica*.

Toyo Ito – who alongside Tadao Ando is the most important standard-bearer of contemporary Japanese architecture in recent decades – has declared that Fujimoto is arguably the most important architect at the beginning of the twenty-first century. He wrote that 'in Fujimoto's architecture the space of human relationships is geared more to the outside'. This applies to House NA as much as it does to his urban design project in China, a proposal for a city that resembles a monumental crystal and in which there are no longer squares, only ramps and niches, in which public life builds its nests.

In Japan – at least since the fine, clear and completely no-frills Sukiya style of the seventeenth-century (best known from the classical tea houses) – reduction has ceased to be considered a failure and instead is grasped as liberation from unnecessary ballast. Fujimoto's buildings are clearly in this lineage; they demonstrate that density need not spawn claustrophobia and compulsive restriction, since the art of concentration creates new freedoms.

Unimaginative architects like to insist that buildings cannot change a society, which is usually an excuse for their own inability. If architecture can't change anything anyway, then it can't do any harm when it looks boring. Fortunately, this depressing phase in architectural history – when architects justified their well-tempered unimaginativeness by claiming that architectural utopias had only brought misery to cities and their inhabitants – is over. Fujimoto shows that this need not be the case.

His architecture – and in this sense, it is political – bears traits of a societal model in architecture that provides new spaces for new experiences, needs and rituals. On the roof of the residential boxes, to which a small ladder leads, you can breakfast in the morning sun, meet other inhabitants and chat with them. Thus a small utopia arises beyond the nuclear family, one that differs from flat shares by giving everyone their own micro-house complete with bathroom and cooker. House before House is a model for an architecture that accommodates larger groups of friends, cross-family residential clusters, singles, pensioners, and business travellers. At heart, all these avant-garde architectures rediscover an old quality of the city, one that got lost with the reduction of residential architecture to boxes for nuclear families. In the various new Japanese buildings, a notion of community and an idea of hospitality resurfaces, going beyond the atomized family. We see spaces where children from different families can play together, where strangers passing through and migrant labourers can sit down next to locals, where the neighbours look after old people requiring care, and meals in the courtyard are shared not just by father, mother, child and granny, but often by as many as twenty people in a space that oscillates between a small public square and a communal kitchen.

Social change calls for more flexible spaces that can absorb a widowed grandfather who requires care but neither wishes to go into an institutional home nor place a strain on his family; that can cater to the manager who is only in the city two days a week but does not want to sleep in an anonymous hotel room and wishes to experience something of the life and people in the city whose guest he is; that can be a home for the friend who has lost his job and can no longer afford a large flat; that can house the graduate who has completed her studies and needs to move back home temporarily while hunting for a job. To date, all these people have been considered problems who disturb the idyll of the classical house. Fujimoto's architecture points in a different direction. In House before House the rooms drift apart and nature grows into the corridors to create new microspaces between the residential cells. The house is taken apart, and with it the battery of concepts used to conceive it, initiating instead a new form of dwelling, of being public or being on one's own.

Sou Fujimoto Architects office, 2013

ON THE MAKING
OF A CLOUD

Julia Peyton-Jones

As I write, I am looking at a small white porcelain object that is half bird, half animal, decorated with an image of a painted flower and Japanese script and attached to a red and white cord that is not long enough to suspend from a shelf, a tree or a hook. For all its oddness, it is a beguiling thing and important to me for what it represents. This small creature was a gift given to me on 2 January 2013 in a restaurant when I was in Tokyo. Earlier that day I had called Toyo Ito, who designed the Serpentine Gallery Pavilion in 2002, from Sou Fujimoto's office. I was delighted and surprised when Ito answered the telephone despite the fact that this was a holiday in Japan, and even more surprised when he immediately suggested that we meet that very evening and that we invite Fujimoto, along with Kazuyo Sejima and Ryue Nishizawa of SANAA (designers of the 2009 Pavilion) to join us.

The five of us duly gathered at the appointed time in front of a restaurant that any non-Tokyo resident would have passed unnoticed, and were shown into a private wooden-panelled room where we had the most convivial, enjoyable and amusing dinner. Around the table sat the three generations of Japanese architects with whom the Serpentine has had the great good fortune to work. I announced that I was in the presence of the grandfather (Ito), the parents (Sejima and

Models for Serpentine Gallery Pavilion, 2012

Nishizawa) and the son (Fujimoto) of Japanese architecture. The conversation was broad, ranging from architecture to travel to gossip, and many photographs were taken. The evening underscored for me the true spirit of the commission of the Serpentine Pavilion, where, on all sides, a great leap of faith is made, a commitment forged, a miracle achieved and, in spite of some testing and occasionally hair-raising moments, a structure of enormous accomplishment is installed each year on the Serpentine Gallery's lawns in Kensington Gardens for a period of four months.

Fujimoto's first engagement in person at the Serpentine had not been an auspicious one. We had sent him a rather obtuse letter in November 2012, asking him to come to London to discuss the Pavilion, but failing to make our precise intentions clear. I was late for the meeting and by the time I arrived, assuming that he had already been invited to design the 2013 Pavilion, I joined the conversation as if this important matter had already been resolved. My questions ranged from the practical to the logistical, the process to the vision. It was only after an hour of Fujimoto's curious and considered replies that the penny dropped and I realised that the invitation had not in fact been made. It was a moment of great hilarity and the moment when we discovered in each other a resounding sense of humour and an appreciation of the absurd that came to characterise our exchanges, which began in earnest with my subsequent trips to Tokyo and continued to develop throughout the project.

As soon as my Co-Director at the Serpentine Gallery Hans Ulrich Obrist, the Head of Programmes Jochen Volz and I had decided to invite Fujimoto to design the Pavilion, there had been the inevitable sense of urgency that accompanies these commissions, but our great geographical distance from him and his team eventually began to take its toll on the realisation of the project. Following numerous telephone conversations and email exchanges, I found myself in Tokyo over the New Year. The purpose of my visit was to understand Fujimoto's scheme more thoroughly, and to establish whether or not we could make his structure within the time scale and within our budget. Part of the challenge was to be the bridge between Fujimoto's office and the team in London, acting as interpreter and translator, conveying the engineering aspects of his design, and testing the concept in terms of the challenges of the Serpentine's location. It is not unusual for the design to go through a number of iterations as we review the architect's hypotheses about what is possible. This project was no different: an early scheme metamorphosed into an auditorium, which turned into a ring, which developed into a gridded cloud. The practical considerations are an essential part of a pavilion's success, and to ensure that it can be built it is absolutely necessary to explore the scheme from every possible angle.

Sou Fujimoto Architects office, 2012

Visiting Fujimoto's studio turned out to be an engaging and stimulating process. I found his office on the top floor of a warehouse in the Shinjuku-ku district, accessed by a goods lift that would not have been out of place in New York. His team sat at simple trestle tables, on each of which was a computer. In a narrow corridor, there were boards leaning against the wall with projects pinned on them. The models of the Serpentine Pavilion, in a number of sizes, took up almost a quarter of the office space. The overall impression of the design was that it was very simple and curiously lo-tech.

Just as the rectangular modules in Piet Mondrian's 1919 *Composition with Grid 9* draw their dimensions from the rectangular parameters of the canvas surface, Fujimoto's Pavilion is made up of a grid; the layering and meshing of different scales and weights of lines became the starting point for the design. A tartan rug casually thrown across the back of a studio chair illustrated the way in which the grid could be broken or folded, and did not have to conform to a rigid structure. This was also clear from one of the studio's large-scale balsa-wood models, built to represent a combination of 800 mm and 400 mm sections, the smaller pieces made from the larger pieces, broken up with pliers and reshaped with glue. Fujimoto's thinking about the grid is emphatically not a case of linear progression, as it was for Mondrian – and indeed it was fascinating to discover that he was not familiar with the work of Sol Le Witt prior to our conversations. Yet with the completion of the Pavilion it becomes possible to look upon his practice over the last two decades as an exploration of the grid and the spaces it creates, culminating in its total realisation in this work.

Fujimoto's Final Wooden House, completed in Kumamoto in 2008, employs a strict and simple system of formal permutations that create a bewildering visual effect. Cubes and cuboids, the building blocks of the grid, are used in three differing heights and three areas to build an open or closed interior and exterior. From the outside there is a sense of calm and order – a cube formed of large timber beams – but upon entering one finds protruding beams that create irregular platforms and recessions in a carefully choreographed confusion of the formal order. The experience within, however, remains humane and inviting. This is partly an effect of the medium – timber is the warmest of surfaces, and the principle material of the vernacular Machiya townhouses that exist across Japan – but it is also in large measure because the proportions of the human body remain Fujimoto's primary point of departure. Mondrian saw architecture's necessary deferral to the dimensions of the human body as its limitation, but for Fujimoto this is also its liberation. The Final Wooden House seeks not to obstruct the movement of its occupants, but to inspire it by way of a creative adaptation to the conditions of the space.

The Serpentine Pavilion extends the concerns of Final Wooden House by enacting a shift from the density of timber to the varied transparency of the steel grid. The Pavilion becomes an exercise not only in the direct manipulation of space in order to create a field for many varied kinds of behaviour, but also an exercise in the effects of light, and an intricate frustration of the separation of exterior from interior. All this is achieved by way of Fujimoto's interest in the demands and possibilities of the movement of bodies through space. He deploys the discipline and severity of the grid within the verdant surroundings of Kensington Gardens, and yet does not obtrude upon this setting. From certain vantages, in fact, the exterior of the Pavilion seems to dematerialise. This disappearance is mirrored within, in the differing levels of density that admits and obscures the surrounding nature, echoing the variable opacities of woodland and tree canopies.

During the January studio visits the exchange on both sides was rigorous and engaging and included David Glover, our structural engineer. Speaking about past and future projects, it became apparent how much the hand is always present in the preliminary work that Fujimoto performs, whether it is with wood, pliers, glue, cardboard, paper or any other element that can be used to create forms that test an idea or prove a concept. The technology he chooses remains simple; our conversations were also direct and refreshing, clear and straightforward. The degree of focus and commitment was astonishing and the task was undertaken with a spirit of openness and generosity that allowed for fascinating discussions throughout the project, where both sides pressed the other in the spirit of enquiry, knowledge and a better understanding. This is part of the reason why this year's Pavilion remains a source of endless fascination.

Biographies

Born in Hokkaido in 1971, **Sou Fujimoto** is widely acknowledged as being one of the most important architects coming to prominence worldwide. After studying architecture at the Department of Architecture in the Faculty of Engineering at Tokyo University, he established Sou Fujimoto Architects in 2000. In 2012, Fujimoto was awarded the Golden Lion for National Participation at the Venice Architecture Biennale along with Kumiko Inui, Akihisa Hirata and Naoya Hatakeyama.

Fujimoto has completed the majority of his buildings in Japan, with commissions ranging from the domestic (such as Final Wooden House, T House or House NA) to the institutional (such as the Musashino Art University Library at Tokyo University). Following on from his first built work, an occupational therapy building for Seidai Hospital, Fujimoto has produced a number of designs for healthcare institutions, including the Children's Psychiatric Rehabilitation Center in Hokkaido.

Part of a new generation of architects who are reinventing our relationship to the built environment, the work of Sou Fujimoto resists categorisation. The separation of private interior from public exterior spaces is constantly questioned by his interlocking, light weight, flexible designs. With this approach he creates forms that are committed to a playful interaction between user and space. Alongside private residences, such as the well-known House N, his Musashino Art University Library has achieved particular recognition.

Niklas Maak is the editor of the arts section of the *Frankfurter Allgemeine Zeitung* alongside Julia Voss, as well as the publication's artistic director. He is a regular contributor to *Merian* magazine and has taught as a visiting professor in architectural history at the Johann Wolfgang Goethe University in Frankfurt am Main, and at the Universities of Basel and Berlin.

Serpentine Gallery Pavilion 2013
Project Team

Architect
Sou Fujimoto

Architectural Design Team
Nadine De Ripainsel
Keisuke Kiri
Ryo Tsuchie
Haruka Tomoeda
Yibei Liu
Midori Hasuike
Minako Suzuki
Marie de France
Andreas Nordström
Shintaro Honma
Naganobu Matsumura
Hideto Chijiwa

Project Directors
Julia Peyton-Jones with
Hans Ulrich Obrist and
Jochen Volz,
Serpentine Gallery

Project Leader
Julie Burnell with
Amy Brown,
Tom Gillard and
Robertta Marques,
Serpentine Gallery

Project Curators
Sophie O'Brien with
Rebecca Lewin,
Serpentine Gallery

Project Managers
Gareth Stapleton with
Nazma Uddin,
RISE

Structural Engineering
David Glover with
Jon Leach,
Tom Webster,
Harriet Eldred and
Jack Wilshaw,
AECOM

Consultants
Barnaby Collins and
James Penfold,
DP9

Construction
Ted Featonby with
Mick Mead and
Tiff Blakey,
Stage One

Project Advisors
Lord Palumbo, Chairman,
Serpentine Board of Trustees
Zaha Hadid, Architect,
Serpentine Board of Trustees
Colin Buttery, Director of
Parks, The Royal Parks
Westminster City Council
Planning Office
Jenny Wilson,
Westminster City Council
District Surveyor's Office
(Building Control)
Hassan Lashkariani
Westminster City Council
(Licensing Authority)
London Fire and Emergency
Planning Authority
London Region, English Heritage
Friends of Hyde Park and
Kensington Gardens

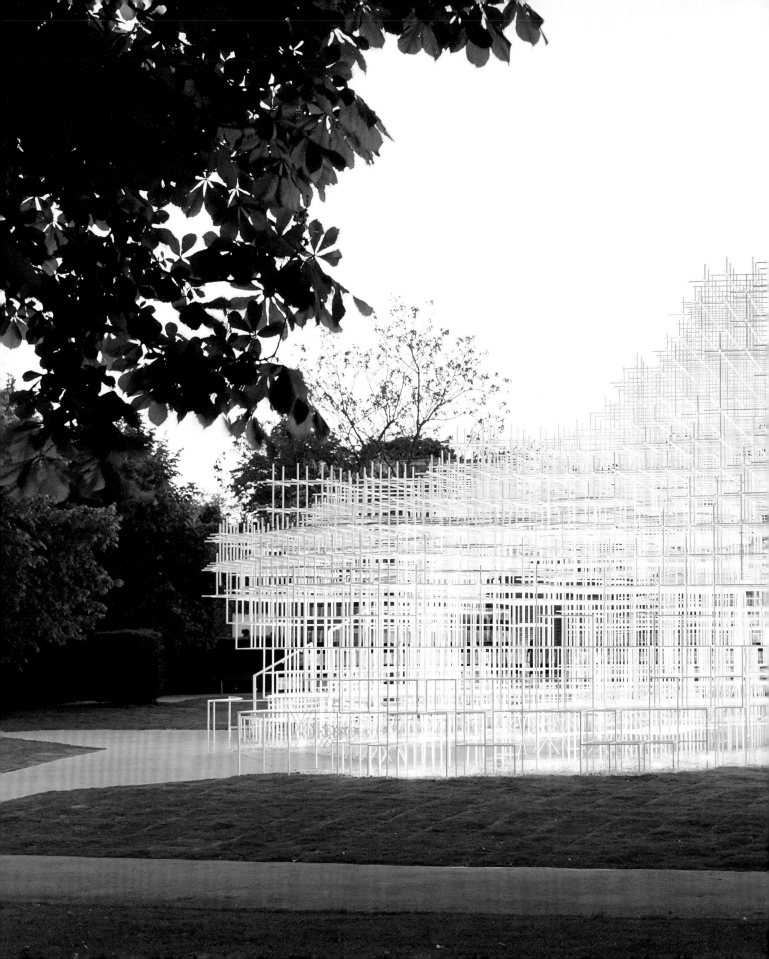

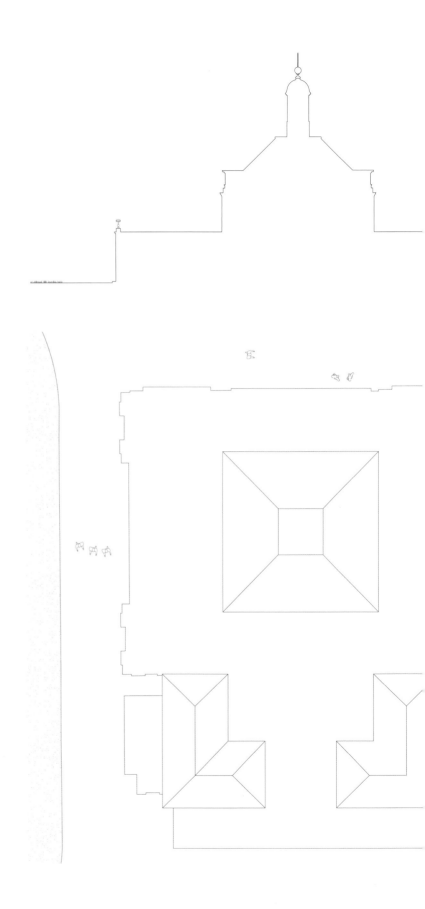

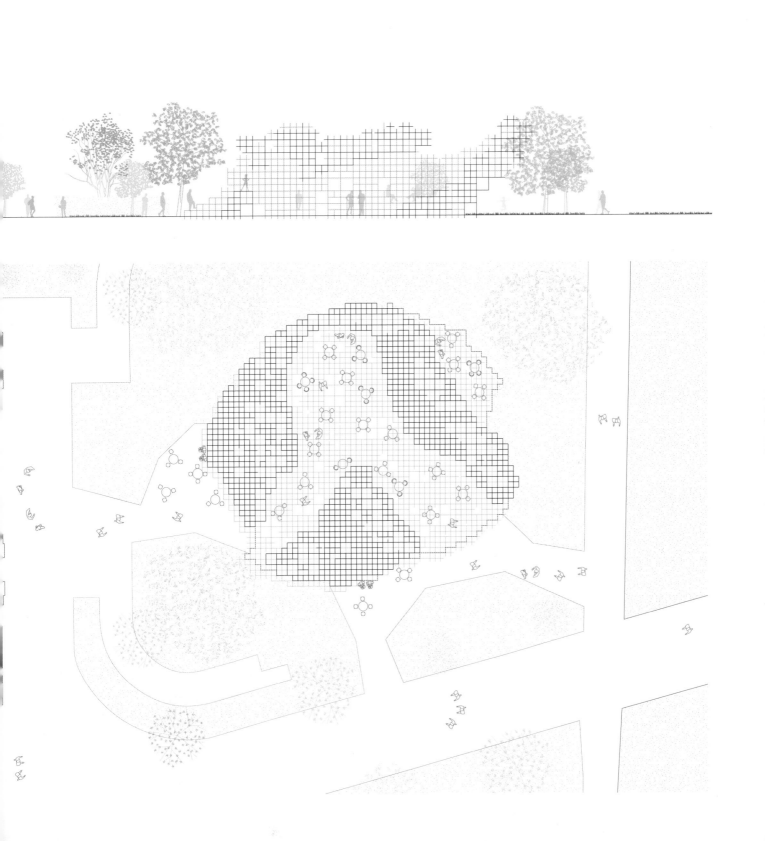

Serpentine Gallery Pavilions
2000–2012

Serpentine Gallery Pavilion 2000
Designed by Zaha Hadid

Eighteen Turns, Serpentine Gallery Pavilion 2001
Designed by Daniel Libeskind with Arup

Serpentine Gallery Pavilion 2002
Designed by Toyo Ito and Cecil Balmond with Arup

Serpentine Gallery Pavilion 2003
Designed by Oscar Niemeyer

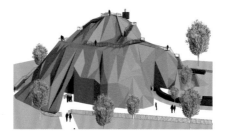

Concept for Serpentine Gallery Pavilion 2004
(unrealised). Designed by MVRDV with Arup

Serpentine Gallery Pavilion 2005
Designed by Álvaro Siza and Eduardo Souto de
Moura with Cecil Balmond and Arup

Serpentine Gallery Pavilion 2006
Designed by Rem Koolhaas and Cecil Balmond
with Arup

Serpentine Gallery Pavilion 2007
Designed by Olafur Eliasson and Kjetil Thorsen

Lilas: an installation by Zaha Hadid Architects 2007
Designed by Zaha Hadid and
Patrik Schumacher

Serpentine Gallery Pavilion 2008
Designed by Frank Gehry

Serpentine Gallery Pavilion 2009
Designed by Kazuyo Sejima + Ryue Nishizawa /
SANAA

Serpentine Gallery Pavilion 2010
Designed by Jean Nouvel

Serpentine Gallery Pavilion 2011
Designed by Peter Zumthor
(Garden design by Piet Oudolf)

Serpentine Gallery Pavilion 2012
Designed by Herzog & de Meuron + Ai Weiwei

Serpentine Gallery Pavilion 2013
Supporters

Sponsored by

With

Media Partner

Advisor

Platinum Sponsors

Gold Sponsors

Silver Sponsors

Bronze Sponsors

Supported by

Additional Support

Funded by

Serpentine Gallery Acknowledgement

Thank you

The generosity of supporters is vital to the Gallery's success. The Serpentine offers innovative ways for all ages to engage with modern and contemporary art, architecture, design and education. In 2012-13, the Gallery raised 81% of its total income through donations, corporate sponsorships, trusts, foundations, endowments and other activities. The Serpentine would like to thank the individuals, trusts, foundations and companies whose generosity and foresight enable the Gallery to realise its acclaimed Exhibition, Architecture, Education and Public Programmes.

Trustees of the Serpentine Gallery
Lord Palumbo *Chairman*
Felicity Waley-Cohen and
Barry Townsley *Co-Vice Chairmen*
Marcus Boyle *Treasurer*
Patricia Bickers
Mark Booth
Roger Bramble
Marco Compagnoni
David Fletcher
Bonnie Greer
Zaha Hadid
Rob Hersov
Colin Tweedy

40th Anniversary Founding Benefactors
Jeanne and William Callanan
The Highmont Foundation
The Luma Foundation

And Founding Benefactors who wish to remain anonymous

Council of the Serpentine Gallery
Rob Hersov *Chairman*

Marlon Abela
Igor and Natasha Akhmerov
Mrs Basil Al-Rahim
Shaikha Paula Al-Sabah
Goga Ashkenazi
Nicolas Berggruen
Mr and Mrs Harry Blain
Mr and Mrs F. Boglione
Mark and Lauren Booth
Jeanne and William Callanan
Michael and Erin Cohen
Michael Conway and
Alison Jacques
Raye Cosbert
Dag Cramér
Aud and Paolo Cuniberti
Carolyn Dailey
Marie Douglas
Russ DeLeon and Serge Tiroche
Griet Dupont
Denise Esfandi
Jenifer Evans
Mark Evans
Nicoletta Fiorucci
and Giovanni Russo
Wendy Fisher
Lawton W. Fitt and James I.
McLaren Foundation
Tim Franks and Andrew Pirrie
Kathrine and Cecilie Fredriksen
Yakir and Elena Gabay
Ingvild and Stephan Goetz
Olivier de Givenchy
Jonathan Goodwin
Mr and Mrs Lorenzo Grabau
Richard and Odile Grogan
Jennifer and Matthew Harris
Susan and Richard Hayden
Mr and Mrs Tim Jefferies
Mrs Kristi Jernigan
Ella Krasner
Mr and Mrs Jonathan Lourie
The Luma Foundation
Leon Max
Usha and Lakshmi N. Mittal
Denis and Yulia Nagi
Dalip and Chandrika Pathak
Catherine and Franck Petitgas
Eva Rausing

The Red Mansion Foundation
Yvonne Rieber
Charlotte Dauphin de La
Rochefoucauld, Comtesse
Charles-Henri de La
Rochefoucauld
Thaddaeus Ropac
Spas and Diliana Roussev
Robin Saunders
Anders and Yukiko Schroeder
David and Simone Sproul
Mr and Mrs Jerome Stern
Ahmed and Cherine Tayeb
Robert Tomei
Andrei and Veronika Tretyakov
Ted Vassilev
Robert and Felicity Waley-Cohen
Bruno Wang
Andrew and Victoria
Watkins-Ball
Mr and Mrs Lars Windhorst
Manuela and Iwan Wirth

And members of the Council who wish to remain anonymous

Council's Circle of the Serpentine Gallery
Eric and Sophie Archambeau
Len Blavatnik
Ivor Braka
Wayne and Helene Burt
Nicholas Candy
Edwin C. Cohen and
The Blessing Way Foundation
Ricki Gail Conway
Alessandro Cajrati Crivelli
Guy and Andrea Dellal
Johan Eliasch
Joey Esfandi
Mala and Oliver Haarmann
The Hon Robert Hanson
Petra and Darko Horvat
Mr and Mrs Michael
Hue-Williams
Michael Jacobson
Dakis Joannou
Jolana Leinson and Petri Vainio
Elena Bowes Marano

Jimmy and Becky Mayer
Viviane and James Mayor
Giles Mackay
Matthew Mellon, in memory
of Isabella Blow
Tamara Mellon
Martin and Amanda Newson
Pia-Christina Miller
J. Harald Orneberg
Stephen and Yana Peel
Silvio and Monica Scaglia
Olivia Schuler-Voith
Mrs Nadja Swarovski-Adams
Phoebe and Bobby Tudor
Hugh Warrender
Beatrice Warrender
Michael Watt
John and Amelia Winter
Michael and Anna Zaoui

And members of the Council's Circle who wish to remain anonymous

Founding Corporate Benefactor
Bloomberg

Exclusive Professional Services Adviser
Deloitte LLP

Platinum Corporate Benefactors
AECOM
Arup
Bloomberg
Diesel
Dornbracht
Hiscox
HP
J.P. Morgan Private Bank
My Beautiful City
Qatar Museums Authority
Rise
UVA
Viabizzuno
Weil, Gotshal & Manges

Gold Corporate Benefactors
COS

Flora Fairbairn
Rebecca Guinness
Katherine Holmgren
Liz Kabler
Dan Macmillan
Bobby Molavi
Jake Parkinson-Smith
Robin Scott-Lawson
Andreas Siegfried
Stan Stalnaker
Christopher Taylor
Rose van Cutsem
Marcus and Alexa Waley-Cohen
Michael Walker
Jonathan Wood

Future Contemporaries:
Members
Jam Acuzar
Noor Al-Rahim
Sharifa Alsudairi
Abdullah Alturki
Kamel Alzarka
Anja and António Batista
Mikael and Leonie Brantberg
Ben Bridgewater
James and Felicia Brocklebank
May Calil
Louise J Cameron
Mary Charteris
Roxanne Cohen
Pilar Corrias
Patrick C. Cunningham
Theo Danjuma
Ruby Danowski
Laetitia Delorme
Niki Dembitz
Sophie Demeyere
Elizabeth R. DuBois
Eleanor A. Edelman
Mrs Selma Feriani
Hugh Gibson
Leila Elizabeth Greiche
Marie Guerlain
Michael Hadjedj
Dr Julia and Christoph
    Hansmeyer
Ivana Hasecic
Matt Hermer
Carolyn Hodler
Kamel Jaber
Karim Jallad
Meruyert Kaliyeva
Zoe Karafylakis Sperling

Chloe Kinsman
Daria Kirsanova
Bettina Korek
Niels Kroner
Christina Gee Kryca
Mans and Abear Larsson
Maged Latif
Kai Lew
James Lindon
Anna Lipskaya
Dan Lywood
Sonia Mak
Jean-David Malat
Ann-Marie Matthijs
Louise McKinney
John Paul Micalleff
Laura Modiano
Fernando J. Moncho Lobo
Isabelle Nowak and Torsten
    Winkler
David Eric Olsson
Sophie Orde
Katharina Ottmann
Jake and Samira Parkinson-
    Smith
Joe Phelan
Carlos and Francesca Pinto
Stephanie de Preux and
Patricia Low
Ollia Alexandra Rarisame
Piotr Rejmer
Valerie Sadoun
Poppy Sebire
James Sevier
Henrietta Shields
Yassi Sohrabi
Dayana Tamenderova
Edward Tang
Monuhar Ullah
Andy Valmorbida
Rachel Verghis
Sam Waley-Cohen
Adam Winogrodzki-Irving
Jonathan and Lucy Wood
Mr and Mrs Nabil Zaouk
Fabrizio D. Zappaterra
Alma Zevi

Benefactors
Cosima and Clemens Aichholzer
Shane Akeroyd
Paul and Kia Armstrong
Jane Attias
Anne Best and Roddy

Kinkead-Weekes
Mr and Mrs John Botts
Marcus Boyle
Mervyn and Helen Bradlow
Benjamin Brown
Mrs Tita Granda Byrne
Lavinia Calza Beveridge
Sadie Coles
Laura Comfort
Carole and Neville Conrad
Mr and Mrs Colin David
Mr and Mrs Christopher Didizian
Mike Fairbrass
Hala Fares and Noor Fares
Heidi Ferid-Hands
Hako and Dörte, Graf and Gräfin
    von Finckenstein
David and Jane Fletcher
Jane and Richard Found
Eric and Louise Franck
Alan and Joanna Gemes
David Gill
Dimitri J. Goulandris
Richard and Judith Greer
Louise Hallett
Jeremy Hargreave
Susan Harris
Timothy and Daška Hatton
Maria and Stratis Hatzistefanis
Alison Henry-Davies
Mrs Christine Johnston
Marcelle Joseph and
    Paolo Cicchiné
James and Clare Kirkman
Mr and Mrs Lahoud
Geraldine Larkin
Julie Lee
Anne and Sydney Levinson
George and Angie Loudon
Cary J. Martin
Penny Mather
Ruth and Robert Maxted
Viviane and James Mayor
Warren and Victoria Miro
Robin Monotti Graziadei
Dr Maigaelle Moulene
Paul Munford
Georgia Oetker
Jacqueline O'Leary
Desmond Page and Asun
    Gelardin
Maureen Paley
Dominic Palfreyman
Julia Peyton-Jones OBE

Mrs Janaki Prosdocimi
Ashraf Qizilbash
Bruce and Shadi Ritchie
Kimberley Robson-Ortiz
Jacqueline and Nicholas Roe
Fabio Rossi
James Roundell
Joana and Henrik Schliemann
Susan L. Schwartz
Nick Simou and Julie Gatland
Bina and Philippe von
    Stauffenberg
Simone and Robert Suss
The Thames Wharf Charity
Britt Tidelius
Gretchen and Jus Trusted
Alexander V. Petalas
Audrey Wallrock
Lady Corinne Wellesley
Alannah Weston
Helen Ytuarte White
Dr Yvonne Winkler
Mr Ulf Wissen
Henry and Rachel Wyndham
Mr and Mrs Nabil Zaouk
Jean-David Zorbibe

And Learning Council, Patrons,
Future Contemporaries and
Benefactors who wish to remain
anonymous

Supported by
Arts Council England
The Royal Parks
Westminster City Council

Serpentine Gallery
Staff List

Directors

Director, Serpentine Gallery
and Co-Director, Exhibitions
and Programmes
Julia Peyton-Jones

Co-Director, Exhibitions
and Programmes and Director
of International Projects
Hans Ulrich Obrist

Executive Support
Chief Operating Officer
Jackie McNerney

Operations & Planning Officer
Andrew Fletcher

Executive Assistant to Julia
Peyton-Jones
Katie Doubleday

Research Assistant
Nick Salmon

Personal Assistant, Director's
Office
Jennifer Taylor

Executive Assistant to Hans
Ulrich Obrist
Lorraine Two

Commerce

Head of Commerce
Gregory Krum

Communications
Head of Communications
Rose Dempsey

Head of Media Relations
Miles Evans

Web Editor
Will Barrett

Web Content Editor
Igor Toronyi-Lalic

Communications Print Manager
Mary Lehner

Communications Co-ordinator
Varind Ramful

Development & Events

Head of Campaigns and
Special Projects
Andrew McGowan

Head of Events
Michelle Anselmo

Special Events Consultant
Charlotte Wolseley Brinton

Special Events Assistant
Nicky Gray

Head of Grants, Trusts
& Foundations
Emma Claridge

Trusts and Foundations
Coordinator
Sarah Hardie

Editions and Information
Manager
Tom Harrisson

Corporate Development Manager
Charlie Hill

Development Administrator
Mary Brooke Dreux

Development Co-ordinator
Poppy Parry

Head of Individual Giving
Arianne Lovelace

Membership Manager,
Individual Giving
Rachel Stephens

Events Organiser
Duncan Welsh

Prints Assistant
Matthew Johnstone

Facilities

Facilities Manager
Rohan Perera

Facilities Assistant
Rene Songui

Finance

Head of Finance
Yasmin Younis

Financial Accountant
Elizabeth Walsh

Finance Officer
Annand Wiffen

Human Resources

Head of Human Resources
Gwen Barry

Human Resources Assistant
Tom Gillard

Programmes

Head of Programmes
Jochen Volz

Assistant Curator
Claire Feeley

Gallery Manager
Mike Gaughan

Assistant Gallery Manager
Matt Glenn

Projects Curator
Janna Graham

Assistant Projects Curator
Amal Khalaf

Assistant Curator
Rebecca Lewin

Senior Exhibition Curator
Sophie O'Brien

Assistant Curator, Public
Programmes
Lucia Pietroiusti

Senior Exhibition Curator
Kathryn Rattee

Projects

Head of Projects
Julie Burnell

Senior Projects PA
Amy Brown

Projects PA
Robertta Marques

Visitor Services

Visitor Services & Sales
Assistants
Chris Baker
Laoise Meek

Photo Credits

This catalogue is published to accompany the
Serpentine Gallery Pavilion 2013 designed by
Sou Fujimoto, 8 June – 20 October 2013.

Editor Sophie O'Brien
Design Melanie Mues
Pavilion images layout Sou Fujimoto
Assistant editors Melissa Larner and
Rebecca Lewin
Transcription Rebecca Catt

Editorial director Karen Marta
Production The Production Department

ISBN 978-3-86335-408-4
Koenig Books, London

ISBN 978-1-908617-11-8
Serpentine Gallery, London

The Serpentine Gallery is supported by

Unless otherwise stated, all sketches,
drawings, diagrams, composite images and
process photographs © 2013 Sou Fujimoto.

Photographs
Unless otherwise stated, all photographs of the
Serpentine Gallery Pavilion 2013 © Iwan Baan.

Serpentine Gallery

Serpentine Gallery
Kensington Gardens
London W2 3XA
t +44 (0)20 7402 6075
f +44 (0)20 7402 4103
www.serpentinegallery.org

First published by Koenig Books, London,
and the Serpentine Gallery, London

Koenig Books Ltd
at the Serpentine Gallery
Kensington Gardens
London W2 3XA
www.koenigbooks.co.uk

Distribution
Buchhandlung Walther König, Köln
Ehrenstr. 4, 50672 Köln
t +49 (0) 221 / 20 59 6-53
f +49 (0) 221 / 20 59 6-60
verlag@buchhandlung-walther-koenig.de

Switzerland
AVA Verlagsauslieferungen AG
Centralweg 16
CH-8910 Affoltern a.A.
t +41 (44) 762 42 60
f +41 (44) 762 42 10
verlagensservice@ava.ch

UK & Eire
Cornerhouse Publications
70 Oxford Street
Manchester M1 5NH
t +44 (0) 161 200 1503
f +44 (0) 161 200 1504
publications@cornerhouse.org

Outside Europe
D.A.P. / Distributed Art Publishers, Inc.
155 6th Avenue, 2nd Floor
USA-New York, NY10013
t +1 (0) 212 627 1999
f +1 (0) 212 627 9484
eleshowitz@dapinc.com